KT-572-681

A26492

Watts, Barrie
Conker.—(Stopwatch books)
1. Horse-chestnut—Juvenile literature
I. Title II. Series
583'.28 QK495.H65

ISBN 0-7136-2928-2

Published by A & C Black (Publishers) Limited
35 Bedford Row, London WC1R 4JH

Reprinted 1990
Acknowledgements
The artwork is by Helen Senior
The publishers wish to thank Jean Imrie for her help and advice.

Filmset by August Filmsetting, Haydock, St Helens.
Printed in Hong Kong by Dai Nippon Printing Co. Ltd.

Conker

Barrie Watts

A & C Black · London

Here is a conker.

Have you ever been out to look for conkers?

They grow on horse chestnut trees, like the ones in this picture.

Conkers are sometimes called horse chestnuts. They are the seeds of the horse chestnut tree.

This book will tell you how conkers grow.

The tree grows sticky buds.

The horse chestnut tree rests through the winter.

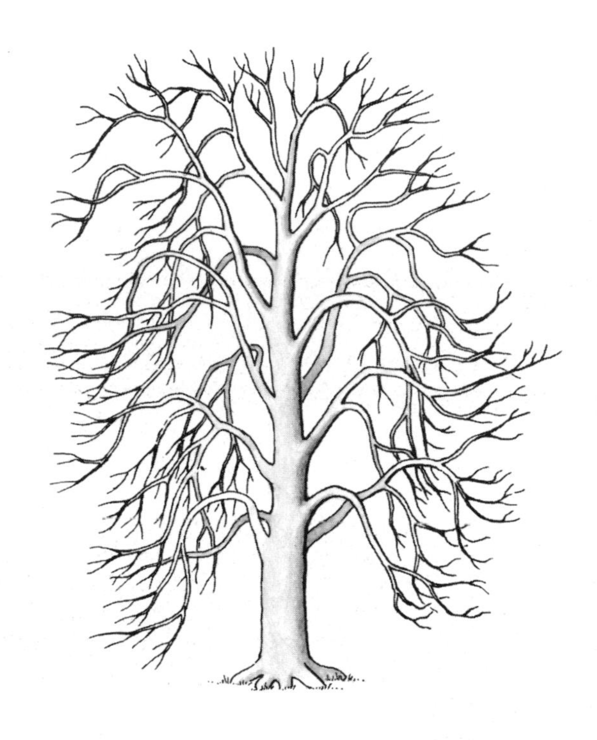

Look at the photograph. At the end of each twig, there is a fat bud. Inside each bud are tiny, crumpled leaves. The leaves are protected from the cold by hard brown scales.

The scales are sticky. This stops insects from eating the buds. Can you see the insects stuck to the buds?

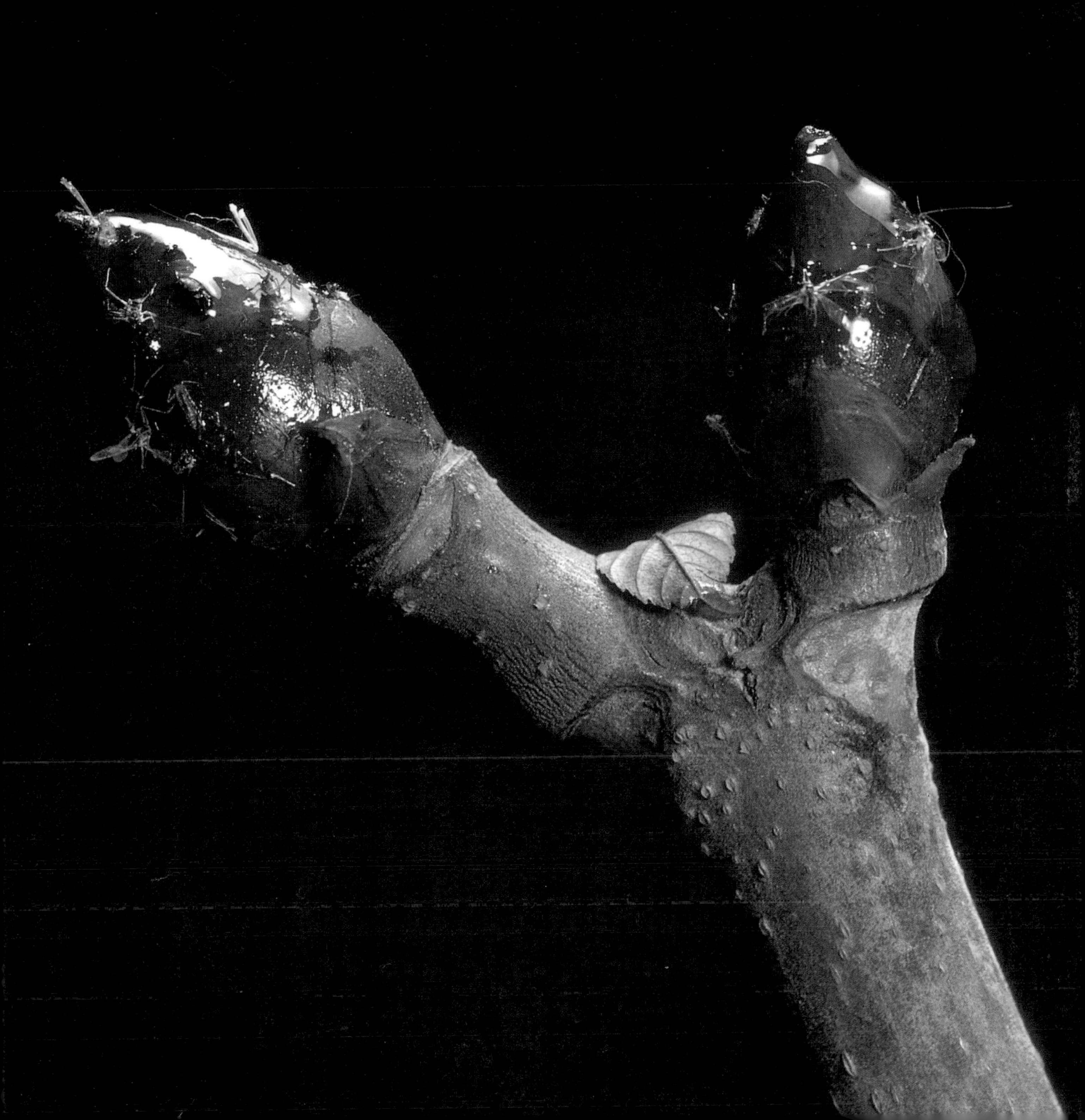

In spring the buds open.

In spring the sticky buds open. The tiny, crumpled leaves start to unfold and grow bigger.

After ten days the leaves have almost unfolded.

Look at the tiny hairs on each leaf. When the leaves are young they are protected by these hairs.
When the leaves get bigger, the hairs fall off.

The leaves are fully grown.

After four weeks the leaves are fully grown. The leaves make food for the growing tree. To do this, they need sunlight, air and water. The leaves open out to catch light and air, and the roots of the tree take in water from the soil.

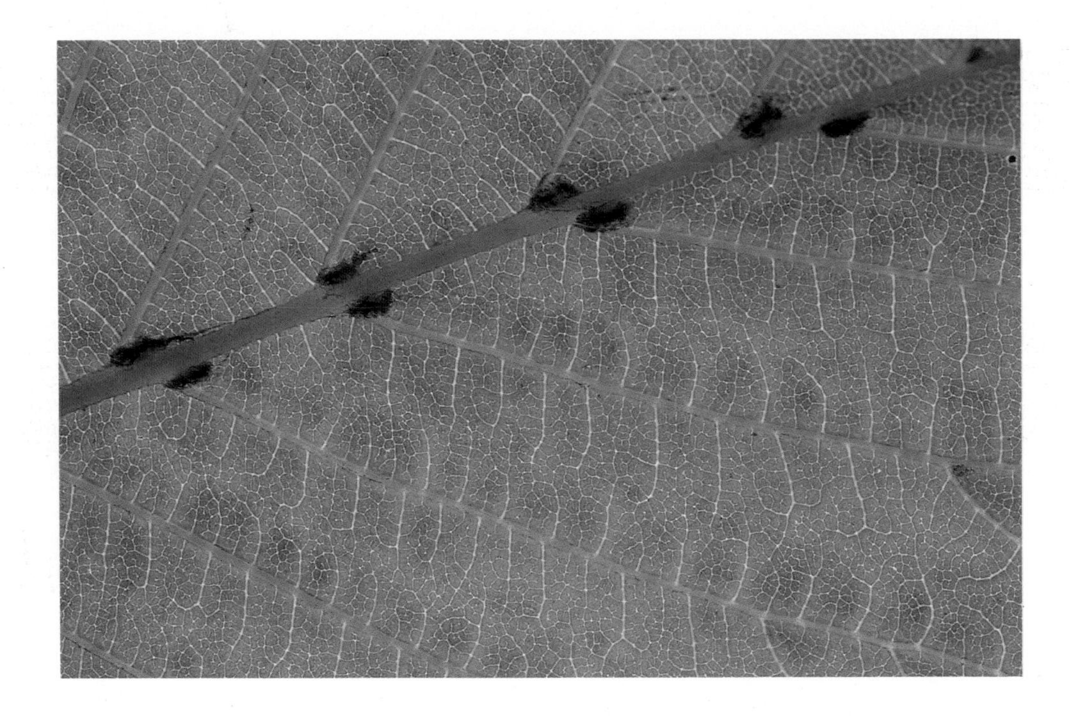

All over each leaf there are tiny tubes called veins. They join up to a big vein in the middle of the leaf. The veins carry food and water to different parts of the tree.

The tree has flowers.

In early summer, the flowers of the horse chestnut tree open. They grow in clusters, called candles. Each candle has up to a hundred tiny flowers.

Inside each flower there are lots of little stalks. The tops of the stalks are covered with orange dust called pollen.

Insects visit the flowers to look for food.

When an insect crawls inside a flower, some pollen may brush on to its body.

A tiny fruit starts to grow.

When the insect visits another flower, some pollen may rub off its body on to the flower. If this happens, a tiny fruit might start to grow inside the flower.

The flower dies, and the fruit gets bigger.
Look at the photograph. Can you see the brown dried-up parts of the flower? Soon they will drop off.

The fruit gets bigger.

After a month the fruits are as big as marbles.

The fruits are hard and spiky. They are poisonous to eat.

Look at the big photograph. This fruit has been
cut in half. Inside the hard green case, there is a soft
white middle where two conkers have started to grow.

Each conker has a runny centre with a thin white skin
around it.

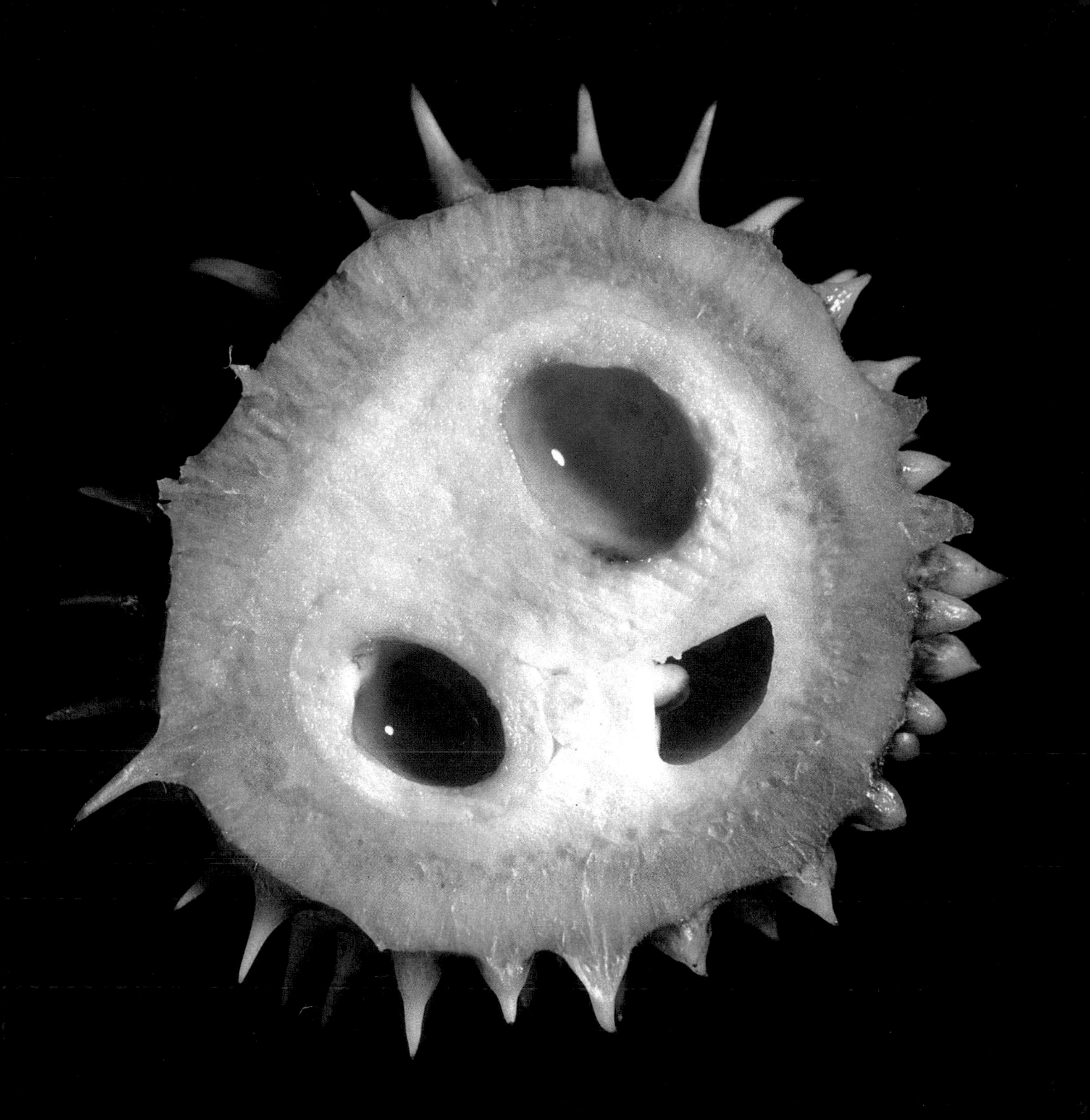

The conkers are nearly ripe.

After ten weeks each fruit has grown as big as a golf ball.

Look at the big photograph. Inside the case, the conkers have grown bigger. The middle of each conker is now green and hard. The white skin has become thinner.

The conkers are nearly fully grown.

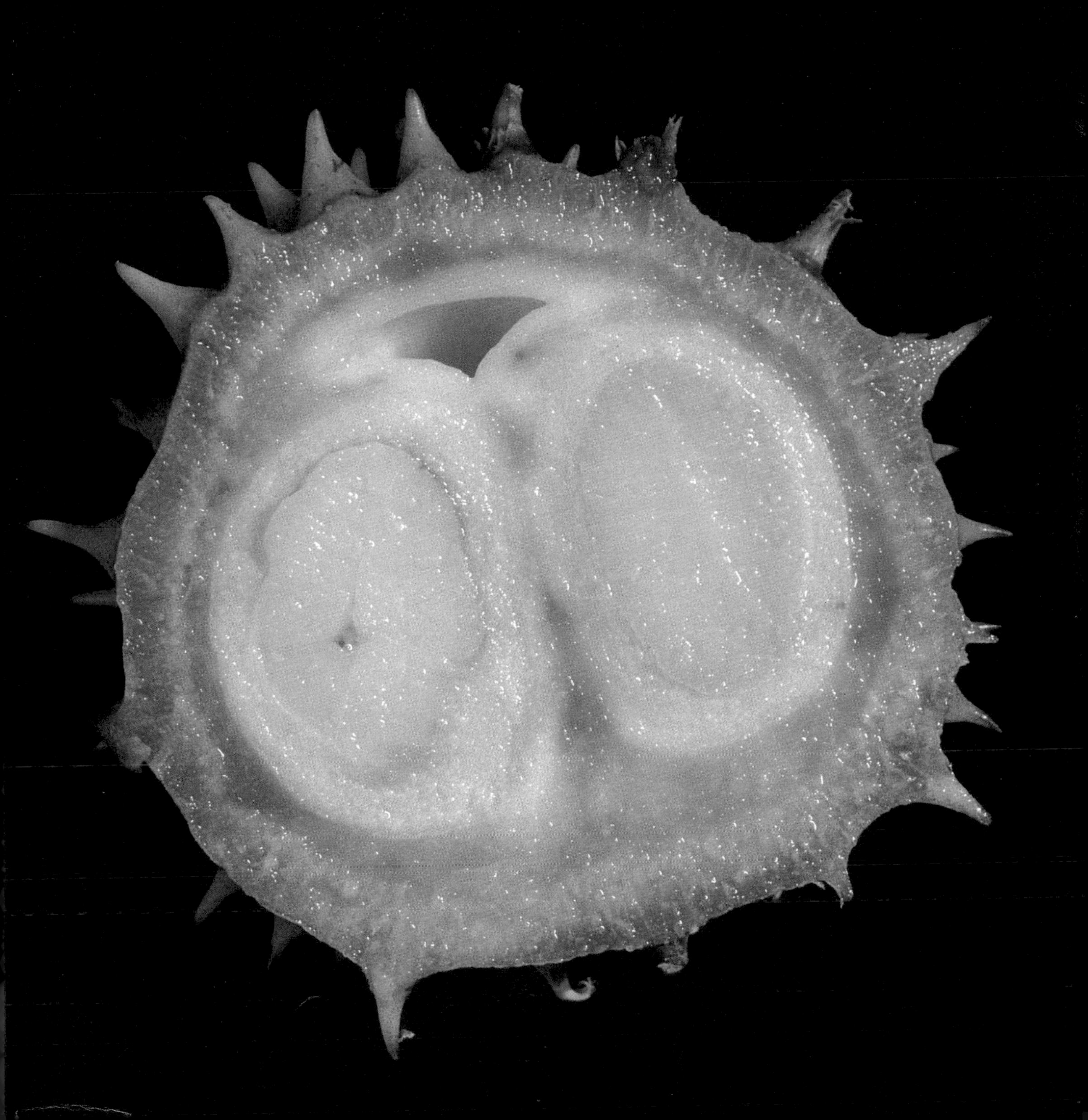

The conkers fall off the tree.

It is autumn and the conkers are ripe. Their skin has turned brown and shiny. As the weather gets colder, the conker case splits open. The conkers are ready to fall from the tree.

These conkers have just fallen to the ground. Some of the conkers are still in their cases.

If a conker falls on to good earth, a tiny tree may start to grow.

The leaves fall off the tree.

In late autumn the tree gets ready for winter.
The leaves stop making food. They dry up and change colour from green to yellow.

When the leaves have dried up they drop off the tree.
A scar is left where the leaf used to be joined to the tree.

Some people say the scar looks like a horseshoe.

The tree rests in winter.

The horse chestnut tree rests in winter.
Sticky buds have grown on its branches.

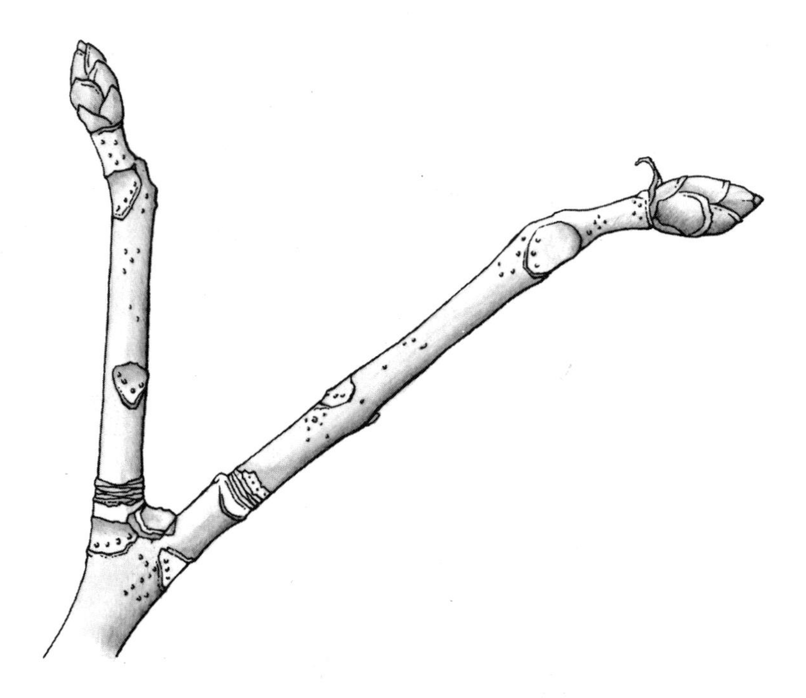

Inside the buds are tiny leaves.

In the spring, the weather will be warmer.
Then the buds will burst open.
What do you think will happen then?

Do you remember how a conker grows?
See if you can tell the story in your own words.
You can use these pictures to help you.

3

6

Try making a conker collection. How many different shapes and sizes can you find under one tree?

Index

This index will help you to find some of the important words in the book.